WITHDRAWAL

KANSAS CITY CHIEFS · SUPER BOWL CHAMPIONS

IV, JANUARY 11, 1970

23-7 VERSUS MINNESOTA VIKINGS

SUPER BOWL CHAMPIONS

KANSAS CITY CHIEFS

AARON FRISCH

CREATIVE EDUCATION

COVER: QUARTERBACK LEN DAWSON

PAGE 2: THE CHIEFS PLAYING DEFENSE IN SUPER BOWL I

RIGHT: COACH HANK STRAM CELEBRATING AFTER SUPER BOWL IV

Published by Creative Education
P.O. Box 227, Mankato, Minnesota 56002
Creative Education is an imprint of The Creative Company
www.thecreativecompany.us

Book and cover design by Blue Design (www.bluedes.com)
Art direction by Rita Marshall
Printed by Corporate Graphics in the United States of
America

Photographs by Dreamstime (Rosco), Getty Images (Vernon
Biever/NFL, Rich Clarkson/Sports Illustrated, Focus On
Sport, Rod Hanna/NFL, Tom Hauck, Andy Hayt, Walter Iooss
Jr./Sports Illustrated, Dave Kaup/AFP, Darryl Norenberg/
NFL, Panoramic Images, Tim Umphrey)

Library of Congress Cataloging-in-Publication Data

Frisch, Aaron.
Kansas City Chiefs / by Aaron Frisch.
p. cm. — (Super Bowl champions)
Includes index.
Summary: An elementary look at the Kansas City Chiefs
professional football team, including its formation in
Dallas in 1960, most memorable players, Super Bowl
championship, and stars of today.
ISBN 978-1-60818-020-2
1. Kansas City Chiefs (Football team)—History—Juvenile
literature. I. Title. II. Series.

GV956.K35 F75 2011
796.332'6409778411—dc22   2009053499

CPSIA: 040110 PO1141

First Edition
9 8 7 6 5 4 3 2 1

CONTENTS

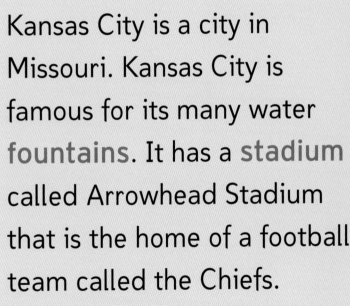

Kansas City is a city in Missouri. Kansas City is famous for its many water **fountains**. It has a **stadium** called Arrowhead Stadium that is the home of a football team called the Chiefs.

CHIEFS FACTS

First season:
1960

Conference/division:
American Football Conference, West Division

Super Bowl championship:
IV, January 11, 1970
23-7 versus Minnesota Vikings

Training camp location:
River Falls, Wisconsin

NFL Web site for kids:
http://nflrush.com

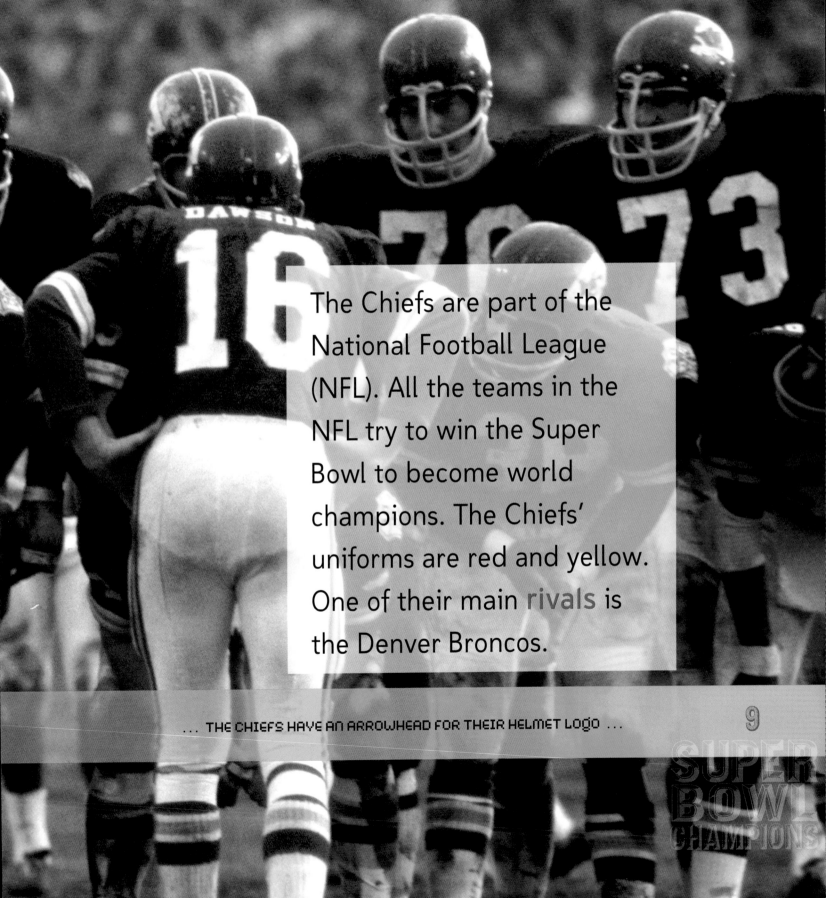

The Chiefs are part of the National Football League (NFL). All the teams in the NFL try to win the Super Bowl to become world champions. The Chiefs' uniforms are red and yellow. One of their main rivals is the Denver Broncos.

SUPER BOWL CHAMPIONS

The Chiefs played their first season in 1960. They were called the Texans at first and played in Dallas, Texas. They were part of a different **league** called the American Football League (AFL) then. In 1962, the Texans won the AFL championship.

11

SUPER BOWL CHAMPIONS

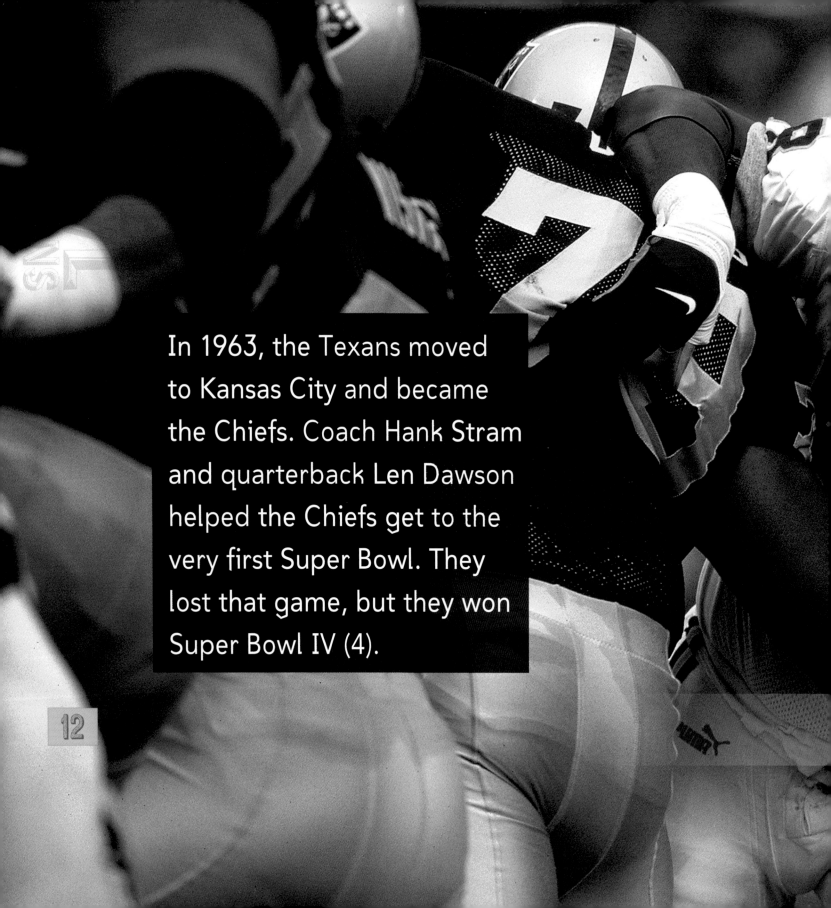

In 1963, the Texans moved to Kansas City and became the Chiefs. Coach Hank Stram and quarterback Len Dawson helped the Chiefs get to the very first Super Bowl. They lost that game, but they won Super Bowl IV (4).

The Chiefs were not a great team in the 1970s. But in the 1980s, they added talented players like linebacker Derrick Thomas. The Chiefs started winning more games again.

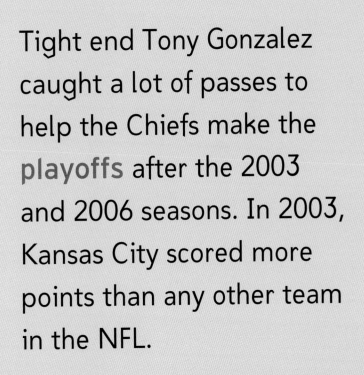

Tight end Tony Gonzalez caught a lot of passes to help the Chiefs make the **playoffs** after the 2003 and 2006 seasons. In 2003, Kansas City scored more points than any other team in the NFL.

... TONY GONZALEZ CAUGHT 916 PASSES PLAYING FOR KANSAS CITY ...

Two of the Chiefs' first stars were Otis Taylor and Willie Lanier. Taylor was a tall wide receiver who helped Kansas City win Super Bowl IV. Lanier was a strong linebacker who played in the **Pro Bowl** eight straight years.

... OTIS TAYLOR (LEFT) AND WILLIE LANIER (RIGHT) ...

17

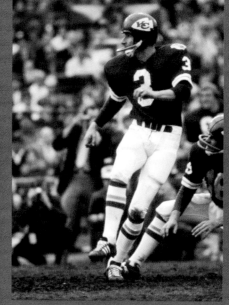

Kicker Jan Stenerud played for the Chiefs for 13 seasons. Some people think he was the best NFL kicker ever. Will Shields was another Kansas City star. He was a powerful guard.

SUPER BOWL CHAMPIONS

... JAN STENERUD (LEFT) AND WILL SHIELDS (RIGHT) ...

The Chiefs added fast wide receiver Dwayne Bowe in 2007. He caught 86 passes in 2008. Kansas City fans hoped that he would help lead the Chiefs to their second Super Bowl championship!

 ... DWAYNE BOWE WAS HARD TO CATCH WHEN HE HAD THE BALL ...

WHY ARE THEY CALLED THE CHIEFS?

The Chiefs were called the Texans at first because they started out in Dallas, Texas. They were renamed when they moved to Kansas City in 1963. A chief is the leader of an Indian tribe. There were once many American Indians in Missouri.

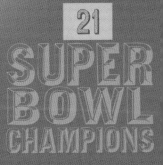

21

SUPER
BOWL
CHAMPIONS

SUPER BOWL CHAMPIONS

GLOSSARY

fountains — structures that make water bubble up or shoot into the air

league — a group of teams that all play against each other

playoffs — games that the best teams play after a season to see who the champion will be

Pro Bowl — a special game after the season where only the NFL's best players get to play

rivals — teams that play extra hard against each other

stadium — a large building that has a sports field and many seats for fans

23

SUPER BOWL CHAMPIONS

INDEX

WITHDRAWAL